Edwin Arnold, Susan Sheridan

Selected Poems from Light of Asia and Light of the World

Edwin Arnold, Susan Sheridan

Selected Poems from Light of Asia and Light of the World

ISBN/EAN: 9783337319779

Printed in Europe, USA, Canada, Australia, Japan

Cover: Foto ©Thomas Meinert / pixelio.de

More available books at **www.hansebooks.com**

ENGLISH CLASSIC SERIES.—No. **98.**

SELECTED POEMS

FROM THE FOLLOWING VOLUMES:

LIGHT OF ASIA.	WITH SA'DI IN THE GARDEN.
LIGHT OF THE WORLD.	LOTUS AND JEWEL.
PEARLS OF THE FAITH.	MISCELLANEOUS POEMS.

BY

SIR EDWIN ARNOLD.

With Introduction and Explanatory Notes

By SUSAN S. SHERIDAN,

High School, New Haven, Conn.

NEW YORK:

EFFINGHAM MAYNARD & CO., PUBLISHERS,

771 BROADWAY AND 67 & 69 NINTH STREET.

New Series, No. 8. January 25, 1892. Published Semi-weekly. Subscription Price $10
Entered at Post Office, New York, as Second-class Matter.

A Complete Course in the Study of English.

Spelling, Language, Grammar, Composition, Literature.

REED'S WORD LESSONS—A COMPLETE SPELLER.
REED'S INTRODUCTORY LANGUAGE WORK.
REED & KELLOGG'S GRADED LESSONS IN ENGLISH.
REED & KELLOGG'S HIGHER LESSONS IN ENGLISH.
REED & KELLOGG'S ONE-BOOK COURSE IN ENGLISH.
KELLOGG'S TEXT-BOOK ON RHETORIC.
KELLOGG'S TEXT-BOOK ON ENGLISH LITERATURE.

In the preparation of this series the authors have had one object clearly in view—to so develop the study of the English language as to present a complete, progressive course, from the Spelling-Book to the study of English Literature. The troublesome contradictions which arise in using books arranged by different authors on these subjects, and which require much time for explanation in the school-room, will be avoided by the use of the above "Complete Course."

Teachers are earnestly invited to examine these books.

EFFINGHAM MAYNARD & CO., PUBLISHERS,

771 Broadway, New York.

SIR EDWIN ARNOLD, M.A., K.C.I.E., C.S.I.

SIR EDWIN ARNOLD, poet, Sanskrit scholar, and journalist, was born June 10, 1832 : and was educated at King's School, Rochester ; at King's College, London ; and at Oxford. In 1852 he won the Newdegate prize for English verse. After graduation he was appointed second master of King Edward VI.'s College at Birmingham, but was soon after sent to India as principal of the Sanskrit college at Poonah, in the presidency of Bombay, with a fellowship in the University of Bombay. He held this position from 1857 to 1861. Then, returning to England, he became one of the editorial staff of the *Daily Telegraph*, with which paper he has ever since been connected.

He is a constant and earnest writer, and one of the best authorities on Eastern questions. He it was who suggested the sending of the George Smith expedition to Assyria ; at his suggestion, too, the *Daily Telegraph* co-operated with the *New York Herald* in equipping Stanley for his explorations in Africa.

Among his works are the following : *Griselda*, a drama ; numerous translations from the Greek and Sanskrit ; an annotated copy of the *Hitopadeça*, with a vocabulary in English, Sanskrit, and Mahratti ; a translation of the *Gita-Govinda* under the title *The Indian Song of Songs ;* a translation of the Hitopadeça under the title *The Book of Good Counsels ; The Education of India ;* and *The History of the Administration of India under the late Marquis of Dalhousie.* He is probably best known for his poems *The Light of Asia* and *The Light of the World.* The former tells of the life and teaching of Gautama, the founder of Buddhism. The author's purpose is to give to Europeans a fair view of Buddhism as a religious system, and to promote greater sympathy and cordiality among the races of the British Empire. His *Light of*

3

the World, the divine tragedy of the life and death of Christ, comes more closely home to the bosoms of men. His volume of *Indian Poetry* contains translations from the *Mahábhárata* and *Pearls of the Faith.* In the latter he attempts to do for Mohammedanism what he has already done for Buddhism and Brahmanism.

Sir Edwin Arnold married an American lady, grand-niece of the theologian Dr. W. E. Channing.

In the autumn of 1891 he made a tour of the principal cities of the United States, giving readings from his most noted works.

"Never since the throne of English Song was filled by Shakespeare, to whom (*longo intervallo*) Lord Tennyson is a worthy successor, has any single sovereign had such peers as he in Robert Browning, Matthew Arnold, Algernon Charles Swinburne, Dante Gabriel Rossetti, William Morris, and Sir Edwin Arnold. They cannot be said to resemble each other as the Elizabethan poets resembled each other, and it is one of their great distinctions that they do not, each dwelling in his own lordly pleasure-house, and triumphing in his own realm of thought and feeling—Browning in the domain of spiritual tragedy, Arnold in the cloister of scholarly meditation, Swinburne in the halls of stormy harmony, Rossetti in the border-land between things seen and unseen, Morris in a paradise of earthly visions and fantasies, and Sir Edwin in the barbaric splendors of the Orient, the shadowy maze of its mythology, and the mysterious light of its speculation."

One who has seen Sir Edwin in the bosom of his family says : "If you know 'The Light of Asia,' you have the essence of Sir Edwin Arnold's personality :

'Soft speech, and willing service sweetly rendered.'

. . . When any one verged on the personal—and we all talked freely—it was a lesson to hear Sir Edwin suggest some gentle or charitable way of putting the same speech—always deliciously humorous." This writer adds : "When he was last in India, one day a concourse of Indian priests, eighteen hundred in all, assembled to greet him, carpeting with flowers the road on which he walked. The welcome he met with was not short of adoration, and the Indian peoples told him : 'You have made him live again to us! You have said for us what he is to us! Our sweet Lord Buddha!'"

SELECTED POEMS.

The selections here given are taken from the following volumes :

I.

The Light of Asia.

(SELECTIONS.)

" A generation ago little or nothing was known in Europe of this great faith of Asia, which had nevertheless existed during twenty-four centuries, and at this day surpasses, in the number of its followers and the area of its prevalence, any other form of creed. Four hundred and seventy millions of our race live and die in the tenets of Gautama ; and the spiritual dominions of this ancient teacher extend, at the present time, from Nepaul and Ceylon over the whole Eastern Peninsula to China, Japan, Thibet, Central Asia, Siberia, and even Swedish Lapland. . . . . More than a third of mankind, therefore, owe their moral and religious ideas to this illustrious prince, whose personality, though imperfectly revealed in the existing sources of information, cannot but appear the highest, gentlest, holiest, and most beneficent, with one exception, in the history of Thought."—*From Author's Preface.*

BOOK THE FIRST.

The Scripture of the Saviour of the World,
Lord Buddha—Prince Siddârtha styled on earth—

---

2. Gautama was his personal name, given to him at the name-giving ceremony. When he attained perfect wisdom, he assumed the title *Buddha* —"the Enlightened." All other names are epithets: *Siddartha* means "one who has fulfilled the object (of his coming);" *Tathâgato* means "who comes and goes as his predecessors."

5

In Earth and Heavens and Hells Incomparable,
All-honored, Wisest, Best, most Pitiful;
The Teacher of Nirvâna and the law.

Thus came he to be born again for men.

Below the highest spheres four Regents sit   5
Who rule our world, and under them are zones
Nearer, but nigh, where saintliest spirits dead
Wait thrice ten thousand years, then live again ;
And on Lord Buddha, waiting in that sky,
Came for our sakes the five sure signs of birth,   10
So that the Devas knew the signs, and said,
"Buddha will go again to help the World."
"Yea!" spake He, "now I go to help the World
This last of many times ; for birth and death
End hence for me and those who learn my Law.   15
I will go down among the Sâkyas,
Under the southward snows of Himalay,
Where pious people live and a just King."
That night the wife of King Suddhôdana,
Maya the Queen, asleep beside her Lord,   20
Dreamed a strange dream ; dreamed that a star from heaven—
Splendid, six-rayed, in color rosy-pearl,
Whereof the token was an elephant
Six-tusked and whiter than Vahuka's milk,—
Shot through the void and, shining into her,   25
Entered her womb upon the right.   Awaked,
Bliss beyond mortal mother's filled her breast,
And over half the earth a lovely light
Forewent the morn.   The strong hills shook ; the waves
Sank lulled ; all flowers that blow by day came forth   30
As 'twere high noon ; down to the farthest bells
Passed the Queen's joy, as when warm sunshine thrills

11. **Deva** or **Dev** (Hind. mythology).—A god: a deity; an idol; a king.
16. **Sâkyas.**—An Aryan clan, seated during the fifth century B.C. on the bank of the Kohâna, about 100 miles north of the city of Benares, and about 50 miles south of the foot of the Himalayas.
19. **Suddhôdana.**—Chief of the tribe of the Sâkyas, and rajah of Kapila-vastu (placed somewhere on the confines of Oude and Nepaul).

Wood-glooms to gold, and into all the deeps
A tender whisper pierced. "Oh ye," it said,
" The dead that are to live, the live who die,
Uprise, and hear, and hope ! Buddha is come !"

In this wise was the holy Buddha born.   5

Queen Maya stood at noon, her days fulfilled,
Under a Palsa in the Palace-grounds,
A stately trunk, straight as a temple-shaft,
With crown of glossy leaves and fragrant blooms ;
And, knowing the time come—for all things knew—   10
The conscious tree bent down its boughs to make
A bower about Queen Maya's majesty,
And Earth put forth a thousand sudden flowers
To spread a couch, while, ready for the bath,
The rock hard by gave out a limpid stream   15
Of crystal flow. So brought she forth her child
Pangless—he having on his perfect form
The marks, thirty and two, of blessed birth ;
Of which the great news to the Palace came.
But when they brought the painted palanquin   20
To fetch him home, the bearers of the poles
Were the four Regents of the Earth, come down
From Mount Sumeru—they who write men's deeds
On brazen plates—the Angel of the East,
Whose hosts are clad in silver robes, and bear   25
Targets of pearl : the Angel of the South,
Whose horsemen, the Kumbhandas, ride blue steeds,
With sapphire shields : the Angel of the West,
By Nâgas followed, riding steeds blood-red,
With coral shields : the Angel of the North,   30

---

7. **Palsa.**—The palâça-tree, a familiar leafy forest-tree in India.
23. **Mt. Sumeru** is, according to Buddhist belief, the center of the world,
—as deep in the ocean as it is high above its level. This ocean is inclosed by
a girdle of rocks, within six other concentric oceans with similar girdles.
The whole stands again in the genuine ocean known to men.
27. **Kumbhandas.**—A class of demons.
29. **Nâga** is the name of deified serpents. Their king is Sesha, the sacred
serpent of Vishnu.
30. **Angel of the North.**—*Kubera*, god of wealth; East, *Indra;* West,
Varuna; South, *Yama.* These are the guardians of the world.

Environed by his Yakshas, all in gold,
On yellow horses, bearing shields of gold.
These, with their pomp invisible, came down
And took the poles, in caste and outward garb
Like bearers, yet most mighty gods ; and gods   5
Walked free with men that day, though men knew not:
For Heaven was filled with gladness for Earth's sake,
Knowing Lord Buddha thus was come again.

                        When th' eighth year passed
The careful King bethought to teach his son   10
All that a Prince should learn, for still he shunned
The too vast presage of those miracles,
The glories and the sufferings of a Buddh.
So, in full council of his Ministers,
" Who is the wisest man, great sirs," he asked,   15
" To teach my Prince that which a Prince should know ? "
Whereto gave answer each with instant voice,
" King ! Viswamitra is the wisest one,
The farthest-seen in Scriptures, and the best
In learning, and the manual arts, and all."   20
Thus Viswamitra came and heard commands ;
And, on a day found fortunate, the Prince
Took up his slate of ox-red sandal-wood,
All-beautified by gems around the rim,
And sprinkled smooth with dust of emery,   25
These took he, and his writing-stick, and stood
With eyes bent down before the Sage, who said,
" Child, write this Scripture," speaking low the verse
" Gâyatrî " named, which only High-born hear :—

        Om, tatsaviturvarenyam   30
        Bhargo devasya dhîmahi
        Dhiyo yo na prachodayât.

---

1. **Yakshas** [later Hindoo myth].—Name of a kind of demigods who especially attend on the god of riches.
   29. **Gâyatrî** is the name of a Sanskrit hymn used in morning and evening worship.
   30. **Om.**—A combination of letters invested with peculiar sanctity; a symbol representing the Trinity.

" Acharya, I write," meekly replied
The Prince, and quickly on the dust he drew—
Not in one script, but many characters—
The sacred verse.

But Viswamitra heard it on his face   5
Prostrate before the boy ; " For thou," he cried,
" Art Teacher of thy teachers—thou, not I,
Art Gûrû.   Oh, I worship thee, sweet Prince !
That comest to my school only to show
Thou knowest all without the books, and know'st   10
Fair reverence besides."   Which reverence
Lord Buddha kept to all his schoolmasters,
Albeit beyond their learning taught ; in speech
Right gentle, yet so wise ; princely of mien,
Yet softly-mannered ; modest, deferent,   15
And tender-hearted, though of fearless blood ;
No bolder horseman in the youthful band
E'er rode in gay chase of the shy gazelles ;
No keener driver of the chariot
In mimic contest scoured the Palace-courts ;   20
Yet in mid-play the boy would ofttimes pause,
Letting the deer pass free ; would ofttimes yield
His half-won race because the laboring steeds
Fetched painful breath ; or if his princely mates
Saddened to lose, or if some wistful dream   25
Swept o'er his thoughts.   And ever with the years
Waxed this compassionateness of our Lord,
Even as a great tree grows from two soft leaves,
To spread its shade afar ; but hardly yet
Knew the young child of sorrow, pain, or tears,   30
Save as strange names for things not felt by kings,
Nor ever to be felt.

But on another day the King said, " Come,
Sweet son ! and see the pleasaunce of the spring,

---

1. Acharya.—Priest.
8. Gûrû.—Teacher; " venerable one."

And how the fruitful earth is wooed to yield
Its riches to the reaper ; how my realm—
Which shall be thine when the pile flames for me—
Feeds all its mouths and keeps the King's chest filled.
Fair is the season with new leaves, bright blooms,   5
Green grass and cries of plow-time." So they rode
Into a land of wells and gardens, where,
All up and down the rich red loam, the steers
Strained their strong shoulders in the creaking yoke
Dragging the plows ; the fat soil rose and rolled   10
In smooth dark waves back from the plow ; who drove
Planted both feet upon the leaping share
To make the furrows deep ; among the palms
The tinkle of the rippling water rang,
And where it ran the glad earth 'broidered it   15
With balsams and the spears of lemon-grass.
Elsewhere were sowers who went forth to sow ;
And all the jungle laughed with nesting songs,
And all the thickets rustled with small life
Of lizard, bee, beetle, and creeping things   20
Pleased at the spring-time. In the mango-sprays
The sun-birds flashed ; alone at his green forge
Toiled the loud coppersmith ; bee-eaters hawked
Chasing the purple butterflies ; beneath,
Striped squirrels raced, the mynas perked and picked,   25
The nine brown sisters chattered in the thorn,
The pied fish-tiger hung above the pool,
The egrets stalked among the buffaloes,
The kites sailed circles in the golden air ;
Above the painted temple peacocks flew,   30
The blue doves cooed from every well, far off
The village drums beat for some marriage-feast :
All things spoke peace and plenty, and the Prince
Saw and rejoiced. But, looking deep, he saw

---

25. **Myna.**—Starling; probably the talking starling, or religious grackle,
of India.
28. **Egret.**—A kind of heron.

The thorns which grow upon this rose of life :
How the swart peasant sweated for his wage,
Toiling for leave to live ; and how he urged
The great-eyed oxen through the flaming hours,
Goading their velvet flanks : then marked he, too,   5
How lizard fed on ant, and snake on him,
And kite on both ; and how the fish-hawk robbed
The fish-tiger of that which it had seized ;
The shrike chasing the bulbul, which did chase
The jeweled butterflies ; till everywhere   10
Each slew a slayer and in turn was slain,
Life living upon death. . . . . .
The Prince Siddârtha sighed.   " Is this," he said,
"That happy earth they brought me forth to see ?"
       . . . . . "Go aside   15
A space, and let me muse on what ye show."

So vast a pity filled him, such wide love
For living things, such passion to heal pain,
That by their stress his princely spirit passed
To ecstasy, and, purged from mortal taint   20
Of sense and self, the boy attained thereat
Dhyâna, first step of " the path."

BOOK THE FOURTH.

Then strode he forth into the gloom and cried,
" Channa, awake ! and bring out Kautaka !"

" What would my lord ?" the charioteer replied—   25
Slow-rising from his place beside the gate—
" To ride at night when all the ways are dark ?"

---

9. **Bulbul.**—Nightingale.
22. The key of the whole scheme of Buddhist salvation lies in the four
sublime verities. The first asserts that pain exists; the second, that the
cause of pain is desire or attachment; the third, that pain can be ended by
Nirvâna; the fourth shows the way that leads to Nirvâna. This way con-
sists in eight things: Right Faith; Right Judgment; Right Purpose; Right
Practice; Right Language; Right Obedience; Right Memory; Right Meditation.

"Speak low," Siddârtha said, "and bring my horse,
For now the hour is come when I should quit
This golden prison where my heart lives caged
To find the truth ; which henceforth will I seek,
For all men's sake, until the truth be found."   5

BOOK THE SEVENTH.

Nathless the King broke forth, "Ends it in this
That great Siddârtha steals into his realm,
Wrapped in a clout, shorn, sandaled, craving food
Of low-borns, he whose life was as a God's ?"

"Son ! why is this ?"   10
            "My Father !" came reply,
"It is the custom of my race."
            "Thy race,"
Answered the King, "counteth a hundred thrones
From Maha Sammât, but no deed like this."   15

"Not of a mortal line," the Master said,
"I spake, but of descent invisible,
The Buddhas who have been and who shall be :
Of these am I, and what they did I do."

            ——"And with all lowly love   20
Proffer, where it is owed for tender debts,
The first-fruits of the treasure he hath brought ;
Which now I proffer."
            Then the King amazed
Inquired "What treasure ?" and the Teacher took   25
Meekly the royal palm, and while they paced
Through worshiping streets—the Princess and the King
On either side—he told the things which make
For peace and pureness, those Four noble Truths
Which hold all wisdom as shores shut the seas,   30
Those eight right Rules whereby who will may walk—

15. Maha.—Great.

Monarch or slave—upon the perfect Path
That hath its Stages Four and Precepts Eight,
Whereby whoso will live—mighty or mean,
Wise or unlearned, man, woman, young or old—
Shall soon or late break from the wheels of life   5
Attaining blest Nirvâna.

BOOK THE EIGHTH.

Whilst Buddha spake these things before the King :

The Books say well, my Brothers ! each man's life
    The outcome of his former living is ;
The bygone wrongs bring forth sorrows and woes   10
    The bygone right breeds bliss.

That which ye sow ye reap.   See yonder fields !
    The sesanum was sesanum, the corn
Was corn.   The Silence and the Darkness knew !
    So is a man's fate born.   15

He cometh, reaper of the things he sowed,
    Sesanum, corn, so much cast in past birth ;
And so much weed and poison-stuff, which mar
    Him and the aching earth.

If he shall labor rightly, rooting these,   20
    And planting wholesome seedlings where they grew,
Fruitful and fair and clean the ground shall be,
    And rich the harvest due.

---

6. "**Nirvâna**—is the term denoting the final deliverance of the soul from transmigration. It is, consequently, the last aim of Buddhistic existence, since transmigration is tantamount to a relapse into the evils of the world." At present the best Buddhist scholars incline to the belief that Nirvana does not mean annihilation, but immovable rest.

13. **Sesanum.**—An annual, herbaceous plant, from the seeds of which an oil is expressed; also. the small flattish seeds of this plant, sometimes used for food.

If making none to lack, he throughly purge
   The lie and lust of self forth from his blood ;
Suffering all meekly, rendering for offence
   Nothing but grace and good :

If he shall day by day dwell merciful,   5
   Holy and just and kind and true ; and rend
Desire from where it clings with bleeding roots,
   Till love of life have end :

He—dying—leaveth as the sum of him
   A life-count closed, whose ills are dead and quit,   10
Whose good is quick and mighty, far and near,
   So that fruits follow it.

No need hath such to live as ye name life ;
   That which began in him when he began
Is finished : he hath wrought the purpose through   15
   Of what did make him Man.

Never shall yearnings torture him, nor sins
   Stain him, nor ache of earthly joys and woes
Invade his safe eternal peace ; nor deaths
   And lives recur. He goes   20

Unto Nirvâna. He is one with Life
   Yet lives not. He is blest, ceasing to be.
Om, mani padme, om ! the Dewdrop slips
   Into the shining sea !

---

23. "Om, mani padme, om! is the 'formula of six syllables ' which has acquired much celebrity from the conspicuous part which it plays in the religion of the Buddhists. It is the first subject which the Tibetans and Mongols teach their children, and it is the last prayer which is muttered by the dying man. It is looked upon as the essence of all religion and wisdom, and the means of attaining eternal bliss. Some suppose that it means 'O the jewel in the lotus;' the *jewel* referring to the saint Avalokiteswara himself, and *in the lotus* referring to the belief that he was born from a lotus. It probably means 'Salvation (Om) is the jewel-lotus (mani-padme).'"

The First good Level is *Right Doctrine.* Walk
    In fear of Dharma, shunning all offence ;
In heed of Karma, which doth make men's fate ;
    In lordship over sense.

The Second is *Right Purpose.* Have good-will   5
    To all that lives, letting unkindness die
And greed and wrath ; so that your lives be made
    Like soft airs passing by.

The Third is *Right Discourse.* Govern the lips
    As they were palace-doors, the King within ;   10
Tranquil and fair and courteous be all words
    Which from that presence win.

The Fourth is *Right Behavior.* Let each act
    Assoil a fault or help a merit grow :
Like threads of silver seen through crystal beads   15
    Let love through good deeds show.

———

More is the treasure of the Law than gems ;
    Sweeter than comb its sweetness ; its delights
Delightful past compare. Thereby to live
    Hear the *Five Rules* aright :—   20

Kill not—for Pity's sake—and lest ye stay
    The meanest thing upon its upward way.

Give freely and receive, but take from none
    By greed, or force or fraud, what is his own.

2. " **Dharma** [virtue, duty, law; from *dhri*, to support] comprehends
the revelations, dogmas, and their precepts; and, in a strict sense, cos-
mology and cosmography, mythology, metempsychosis, and the theory of
salvation." The law and scriptures of Buddhism.

3. " **Karma** [Skt. *karman*, act, action, work, fate as the consequence of
acts]. In *Hindoo religion* one's acts considered as determining his lot after
death, and in a following existence; the aggregate of merits and demerits
of a sentient being, in one of his successive existences. Controls destiny of
all sentient beings, not by judicial reward and punishment, but by the result
of cause into effect."

Bear not false witness, slander not, nor lie ;
Truth is the speech of inward purity.

Shun drugs and drinks which work the wit abuse;
Clear minds, clean bodies, need no Sôma juice.

Touch not thy neighbor's wife, neither commit   5
Sins of the flesh unlawful and unfit.

              Here endeth what I write
Who love the Master for his love of us.
A little knowing, little have I told
Touching the Teacher and the Ways of Peace.   10

And how—in fullness of the times—it fell
The Buddha died, the great Tathâgato,
Even as a man 'mongst men, fulfilling all :
And how a thousand thousand crores since then
Have trod the Path which leads whither he went   15
Unto Nirvâna where the Silence lives.

---

4. **Soma juice.**—A drink having intoxicating properties, and playing an important part in sacrifices.
14. **Crore.**—Ten million.

II.

The Light of the World.

(SELECTIONS.)

PROEM.

THE Sovereign Voice spake, once more, in mine ear :
" Write, now, a song unstained by any tear !"

" What shall I write ?" I said.   The Voice replied,
" Write what We tell thee of The Crucified !"

" How shall I write," I said, " who am not meet   5
One word of that sweet speaking to repeat ?"

" It shall be given unto thee !   Do this thing !"
Answered the Voice : " Wash thy lips clean and sing !"

AT BETHLEHEM.

So—or in such wise—those rude shepherds heard
The Angels singing clear ; when not one word   10
Wiser ones caught that night—solemn and still—
Of their high errand : " Peace ! Good-will ! Good-will !"

    Ah ! think we listened there,
      With opened heart and ear,
And heard, in truth, as these men say they heard,   15
      On flock, and rock, and tree,
      Raining such melody ;
Heaven's love descending in that loveliest word,

" Peace !"　Not at first ! not yet !
Our Earth had to forget
Burden of birth, and travail of slow years ;
　　But now the dark time done !
　　Daylight at length begun !　　　　　　　　5
First gold of Sun in sight, dispelling fears !

　　Peace, pledged, at last, to Man !
　　Oh ! if there only ran
Thrill of such surety through one human soul,
　　Would not the swift joy start　　　　　　10
　　From beating heart to heart,
Lighting all lands ; leaping from pole to pole ?

　　Peace, Peace—to come ! to be !
　　If such were certainty
Far-off, at length, at latest, any while,　　　15
　　What woes were hard to bear ?
　　What sorrow worth one tear ?
Murder would soften, black Despair would smile.

　　But, heralded on high,
　　From midnight's purple sky　　　　·　　20
Dropped like the sudden rain which brings the flowers ;
　　Peace !　Aye to dwell with men
　　No strife, no wars ! and, then,
The coupled comfort of those golden hours.

　　Good-will !　Consider this,　　　　　　25
　　What easy, perfect bliss
If, over all the Earth the one change spread
　　That Hate and Fraud should die,
　　And all in amity,
Let go rapine, and wrath, and wrong, and dread !　30

What lack of Paradise
If, in angelic wise,
Each unto Each, as to himself, were dear?
If we in souls descried,
Whatever forms might hide,   5
Own brother, and own sister, everywhere?

All this,—not whispered low
To one heart, full of woe
By reason of blood-reddened fields of Earth,
By sight of Fear and Hate,   10
And policies of state,
And evil fruits which have from these their birth:

But, through their ears, to us
Straitly imparted thus
With pomp of glittering Angels, and their train;   15
And radiance of such light
As maketh mid-day night,
And heavenliest speech of Heaven, not heard again

Till these things come to pass!
Nay, if it be—alas!—   20
A vision, let us sleep and dream it true!
Or—sane, and broad-awake,
For its great sound and sake,
Take it, and make it Earth's, and peace ensue!

  .   .   .   .   .

THE PARABLES.

  .   .   .   .   .

  " Yet most He loved to teach of Love.   25
Wherefore the tale was of a certain man
Dwelling—(we knew him)—by Tiberias,
That had two sons.   And one, the Prodigal,
Had asked his portion, gathered it, and went

To some far country, where he wasted all
In riotous living ; till the ill times fell,
And he had nought, and herded swine, and filled
His belly with the husks.   Sitting at meat
In Simon's house, our Master took this tale,   5
And featly decked it forth with Wisdom's wealth,
Relating how that son 'came to himself'
And cried : 'I will arise and go unto
My Father, and will say that I have sinned,
Sinned against Heaven, and, Father ! before thee,   10
And am not worthy to be called thy Son,   ˏ
Only thy hireling servant !   Make me that !'
Then he arose, and came.   And, oh ! what heart
Throbbed not amongst us, while the Master told
Tenderly,—meaning all the world to hear,—   15
How—yet a long way off—his Father saw,
Saw him, and had compassion ; nay—and ran,
And fell upon his neck, and kissed the boy
Mouth to mouth, Father's lips on Son's lips pressed,
Staying his words of sorrowful self-blame   20
With dear impatience ;—leading us to learn
That God's love runneth faster than our feet
To meet us stealing back to Him and peace,
And kisses dumb our shame, nay, and puts on
The best robe, bidding Angels bring it forth,   25
While Heaven makes festival ; for Angel's meat
Is happiness of man."

.   .   .   .   .

The Great Consummation.

.   .   .   .   .

" We were in Gadara
And—I remember—'twas a summer's eve.
Amid the yellow daisies of the Lake   30

---

28. **Gadara**, the capital of Peræa, in Cœlo-Syria, about four miles eastward of the Sea of Tiberias.   Here, or near here, Christ healed the two men
possessed of devils.   Matt. 8 : 28; Mark 5 : 1.

The children gathered round Him, brought from far
Only that he might touch them.   'Twas that hour
When He rebuked His Twelve, saying, 'Suffer these
To come to Me! the Kingdom is of such!
Who shall receive it as a little child   5
Entereth therein!'   So sitting with a babe
Asleep upon His breast, and on His knee
One round-eyed 'Angel of the Kingdom,' nursed
Full fatherly :—a shallop drove its keel
Sharp on the tinkling shingle, and thence gave   10
My Brother to our band.   For I had told
At Bethany how great the Master was ;
How wise, how holy, how compassionate.
And El'azar sped, running through the reeds ;
And thrust past peasants, mothers, and the Twelve ;   15
And kneeled and prayed : 'Good Master! wherewithal
Shall I gain Life eternal?' Jesus said :
'Call me not good!   None is all good save One!
Thou knowest the Commandments?' at those words
Reciting Moses.   Quoth my brother, then,   20
'All these have I observed from my youth up!'
And Jesus, seeing, loved him ; kissed his head
As Rabbis will when scholars answer well ;
But bade him go his way, sell all his goods,
And give his shekels to the poor, and buy   25
Treasures in Heaven.   Thereat El'azar turned
Sorrowful, for he was a Ruler, owning vines,
Milch-kine and olive-yards.   Yet, that kind kiss
Lay strong upon him ; and he did this thing
And gave much wealth, and lived for better gold,   30
And grew the Master's friend, faithful, and close,
Ministering, when we came into Bethany."

.   .   .   .

      "Then, when the first day of the week was dark,
Alone I wended to His sepulcher,
Bearing fair water, and the frankincense,   35

And linen, that my Lord's sweet body sleep
Well in the rock.   And, while my woful feet
Passed through the gate, and up the paved ascent
Along the Second Wall, over the Hill,
Into that Garden, hard by Golgotha,—   5
The Morning brightened over Moab's peaks,
Touched the great Temple's dome with crimson fires,
Lit Ophel and Moriah rosy-red,
Made Olivet all gold, and, in the pools,
In Hinnom laid a sudden lance of flame.   10
And, from the thorn-trees, brake the waking-songs'
Of little birds ; and every palm-tree's top
Was full of doves that cooed, as knowing not
How Love was dead, and Life's dear glory gone,
And the World's hope lay in the tomb with Him ;   15
Which now I spied,—that hollow in the rock
Under the camphire leaves.   Yet, no guards there
To help me roll the stone ! nay, and no stone !
It lay apart, leaving the door a-gape,
And through the door, as I might dimly see,   20
The scattered wrappings of the Burial-night,
Pale gleams amidst the gloom.   Not waiting, then,—
Deeming our treasure taken wickedly—
I sped ; and came to Peter, and to John ;
And cried : ' Our Lord is stolen from His grave   25
And none to tell where He is borne away !'

---

5. **Golgotha or Calvary.**—A small hill on the north side of Mt. Zion; a place of execution.   Mark 15 : 22; Matt. 27 : 33.
6. **Moab.**—The land eastward and southward of the Dead Sea.   Jer. 48 : 2-39; Amos 2 : 2.
8. **Ophel.**—A part of ancient Jerusalem, outside the south wall of the Temple.   At its foot was the pool of Siloam.   2 Ch. 27 : 3.
8. **Moriah.**—A hill adjacent to Jerusalem.   Here Abraham offered his son.   Gen. 22.   When Solomon built the Temple on it, it became included in the city.   2 Chron. 3 : 1.
9. **Olivet or Mt. of Olives.**—About 625 paces east of Jerusalem.   This is the spot whence Our Saviour ascended into heaven in sight of His apostles.   Luke 19 : 29.
10. **Hinnom.**—A valley or rather ravine on the south side of Jerusalem. This valley was once selected, for its shade and privacy, for the worship of Moloch.   From some point in these cliffs tradition relates that Judas sought his desperate end.   Josh. 15 ; 8.

Thereat, they ran together, came, and saw ;
And entered in ; and found the linen-cloths
Scattered ; the rock-bed empty ; and, amazed,
Back to their house they went.   But I drew nigh   5
A second time, alone ; heart-broken now
The bright day seeming blackest night to me,
The small birds mockers, and the City's noise—
Waking within the walls—hateful and vain.
       .   .   .   .   .   Weeping hard   10
" With these thoughts, like to snake-fangs, stinging me
My left hand on the stone I laid, and shut
The eager sunshine off with my right hand,
Kneeling, and looking in the Sepulcher.
       .   .   .   .   .   " Coming closer, I espied   15
Two men who sate there,—very watchfully—
One at the head, the other at the foot
Of that stone table where my Lord had lain.
Oh ! I say 'men'—I should have known no men
Had eyes like theirs, shapes so majestical,   20
Tongues tuned to such a music as the tone
Wherewith they questioned me : ' Why weepest thou ?'
' Ah, Sirs !' I said, ' my Lord is ta'en away,
Nor wot we whither !' and thereat my tears
Blotted all seeing.   So, I turned to wipe   25
The hot drops off ; and, look !   Another one
Standing behind me, and my foolish eyes
Hard gazing on Him, and not knowing Him !
Indeed, I deemed this was the Gardener
Keeping the Trees and Tomb, so was He flesh ;   30
So living, natural, and made like man
Albeit, if I had marked—if any ray
Of watchful hope had helped me—such a look,
Such Presence, beautiful and pure ; such light
Of loveliest compassion in His face,   35
Had told my beating heart and blinded eyes
WHO this must be.   But I—my brow i' the dust—
Heard Him say softly : ' Wherefore weepest thou ?

Whom seekest thou ?' . . . . .
'Sir,' said I, 'if 'tis thou hast borne Him hence,
Tell me where thou hast laid Him.   Then will I
Bear Him away !' . . . . .
For, while I lay there, sobbing at His feet   5
The word He spake—my Lord ! my King ! my Christ !
Was my name :
                    ' Mary !'

          .   .   .   .   .

                    " No language had I then,
No language have I now ! only I turned   10
My quick glance upward ; saw Him ; knew Him ! sprang
Crying : ' Rabboni !—Lord ! my Lord ! dear Lord !' "

          .   .   .   .   .

                    Peace beginning to be
                    Deep as the sleep of the sea
          When the stars their faces glass   15
                    In its blue tranquillity :
                    Hearts of men upon earth,
                    Never once still from their birth,
                    To rest as the wild waters rest
          With the colors of heaven on their breast !   20

                    Love, which is sunlight of peace,
                    Age by age to increase
          Till anger and hatreds are dead,
                    And sorrow and death shall cease :
                    " Peace on earth and good-will !"   25
                    Souls that are gentle and still
                    Hear the first music of this
                    Far-off, infinite bliss !

III.

Pearls of the Faith.

"It is a custom of many pious Muslims to employ in their devotions a three-stringed chaplet, each string containing thirty-three beads, and each bead representing one of the 'ninety-nine beautiful names of Allah,' whenever this—among many other religious uses—is made of it. The Korân bids them 'celebrate Allah with an abundant celebration,' and on certain occasions—such as during the intervals of the Tarâwih night service in Ramadhân—the Faithful pass these ninety-nine beads of the rosary through their fingers, repeating with each ' Name of God ' an ejaculation of praise and worship. Such an exercise is called *Zikr*, or ' remembrance,' and the rosary *Masba'hah*.

" In the following pages of varied verse I have enumerated these ninety-nine ' beautiful names,' and appended to each—from the point of view of an Indian Mohammedan—some illustrative legend, tradition, record, or comment, drawn from diverse Oriental sources ; occasionally paraphrasing (as closely as possible) from the text of the Korân itself, any particular passage containing the sacred Title, or casting light upon it."—*Extract from Preface.*

8

Call Him Muhaimin, " Help in danger's hour,"
Protector of the true who trust His power.

THE spider and the dove !—what thing is weak
 If Allah makes it strong?
The spider and the dove !—if He protect,   5
 Fear thou not foeman's wrong.

From Mecca to Medina fled our Lord,
 The horsemen followed fast ;
Into a cave to shun their murderous rage,
 Muhammad, weary, passed.   10

Quoth Abu Bekr, " If they see, we die !"
 Quoth Ebn Foheir, " Away !"
The guide Abdallah said, " The sand is deep,
 Those footmarks will betray."

Then spake our Lord, "We are not four, but Five;
  ' He who protects ' is here.
Come ! Al-Muhaimin now will blind their eyes ;
  Enter, and have no fear."

The band drew nigh ; one of the Koreish cried,   5
  "Search ye out yonder cleft,
I see the print of sandalled feet which turn
  Thither, upon the left !"

But when they drew unto the cavern's mouth,
  Lo ! at its entering-in,   10
A ring-necked desert dove sate on her eggs ;
  The maid cooed soft within.

And right athwart the shadow of the cave
  A spider's web was spread ;
The creature hung upon her net at watch ;   15
  Unbroken was each thread.

" By Thammuz' blood," the unbelievers cried,
  " Our toil and time are lost ;
Where doves hatch and the spider spins her snare
  No foot of man hath crossed !"   20

Thus did a desert bird and spider guard
  The blessed Prophet then ;
For all things serve their Maker and their God
  Better than thankless men.

Allah-al-Muhaimin ! shield and save   25
Us, for his sake within that care.

---

17. **Thammuz.**—A Syrian deity (the same as the Phenician *Adon* or *Adonis*), in whose honor a feast was held every year, beginning with the new moon of the month Thammuz or Tanimuz. This month corresponds to part of June and part of July.
21. **Spider.**—One of the Suras of the Korân, the 29th, is named after this insect.
25. **Al-Muhainim.**—The Help in Peril.

35

He is the " Pardoner," and his Scripture hath—
" Paradise is for them that check their wrath,
And pardon sins; so Allah doth with souls;
He loveth best him who himself controls."

KNOW ye of Hassan's slave ?   Hassan the son   5
Of Ali.   In the camp at Ras-al-hadd
He made a banquet unto sheikhs and lords,
Rich dressed and joyous ; and a slave bore round,
Smoking with new-cooked pillaw, Badhan's dish
Carved from rock-crystal, with the feet in gold,   10
And garnets round the rim ; but the boy slipped
Against the tent-rope, and the precious dish
Broke into shards of beauty on the board,
Scalding the son of Ali.   One guest cried,
" Dog ! wert thou mine, for this thing thou shouldst
      howl !"   15
Another, " Wretch ! thou meritest to die."
And yet another, " Hassan ! give me leave
To smite away this swine's head with my sword !"
Even Hassan's self was moved ; but the boy fell
Face to the earth and cried, " My lord ! 'tis writ,   20
' *Paradise is for them that check their wrath.*' "
" 'Tis writ so," Hassan said ; " I am not wroth."
" My lord !" the boy sobbed on, " also 'tis writ,
' *Pardon the trespasser.*' "   Hassan replied,
" 'Tis written—I remember—I forgive."   25
" Now is the blessing of the Most High God
On thee, dear master !" cried the happy slave,
" For He—'tis writ—' *loves the beneficent.*' "
" Yea ! I remember, and I thank thee, slave,"
Quoth Hassan ;—" better is one noble verse   30
Fetched from ' the Book,' than gold and crystal brought
From Yaman's hills.   Lords ! he hath marred the dish,
But mended fault with wisdom.   See, my slave !

I give thee freedom, and this purse to buy
The robe and turban of a Muslim freed."

> *Al-Ghâfir! pardon us, as we*
> *Forgive a brother's injury.*

78

> *Praise Him, Al-Barr! Whose goodness is so great;* 5
> *Who is so loving and compassionate.*

PITY! for He is Pitiful;—a king
Is likest Allah, not in triumphing
'Mid enemies o'erthrown, nor seated high
On stately gold, nor if the echoing sky   10
Rings with his name, but when sweet mercy sways
His words and deeds.   The very best man prays
For Allah's help, since feeble are the best ;
And never shall man reach th' angelic rest
Save by the vast compassion of Heaven's King.   15
Our Prophet once, Ayesha answering,
Spake this: " I shall not enter that pure place,
Even I, except through Allah's covering grace."
Even our Lord (on him be peace !); oh, see !
If *he* besought the Sovereign Clemency,   20
How must we supplicate it ?   Truly thus
Great need there is of Allah's grace for us,
And that we live compassionate !

Hast seen
The record written of Salah-ud-Deen   25
The Sultan ? how he met, upon a day,
In his own city on the public way,

---

3. **Al-Ghâfir.**—The Pardoner.
5. **Al-Barr.**- The Good.
16. **Ayesha.**—The favorite wife of Mahomet's later years.

A woman whom they led to die.   The veil
Was stripped from off her weeping face, and pale
Her shamed cheeks were, and wild her dark fixed eye,
And her lips drawn with terror at the cry
Of the harsh people, and the rugged stones					5
Borne in their hands to break her, flesh and bones ;
For the law stood that sinners such as she
Perish by stoning, and this doom must be ;
So went the wan adulteress to her death.
High noon it was, and the hot khamseen's breath					10
Blew from the desert sands and parched the town.
The crows gasped, and the kine went up and down
With lolling tongues ; the camels moaned ; a crowd
Pressed with their pitchers, wrangling high and loud,
About the tank ; and one dog by a well,					15
Nigh dead with thirst, lay where he yelped and fell,
Glaring upon the water out of reach,
And praying succor in a silent speech,
So piteous were its eyes.   Which when she saw,
This woman from her foot her shoe did draw,					20
Albeit death-sorrowful, and looping up
The long silk of her girdle, made a cup
Of the heel's hollow, and thus let it sink
Until it touched the cool black water's brink ;
So filled th' embroidered shoe, and gave a draught					25
To the spent beast, which whined, and fawned. and quaffed
Her kind gift to the dregs ; next licked her hand,
With such glad looks that all might understand
He held his life from her ; then, at her feet
He followed close, all down the cruel street,					30
Her one friend in that city.

				But the king,
Riding within his litter, marked this thing,
And how the woman, on her way to die,
Had such compassion for the misery					35

---

10. **Khamseen.**—A hot, southerly wind, blowing from the desert.

Of that parched hound : " Take off her chain, and place
The veil once more above the sinner's face,
And lead her to her house in peace !" he said,
" The law is that the people stone thee dead
For that which thou hast wrought ; but there is come,   5
Fawning around thy feet, a witness dumb,
Not heard upon thy trial ; this brute beast
Testifies for thee, sister ! whose weak breast
Death could not make ungentle.   I hold rule
In Allah's stead, who is ' the Merciful,'   10
And hope for mercy ; therefore go thou free—
I dare not show less pity unto thee !"

As we forgive—and more than we—
Ya Barr ! good God ! show clemency.

79

Praise Him, Al-Tawwâb ; if a soul repents,   15
Seven times and seventy times thy Lord relents.

At the gates of Paradise,
Whence the angry Angels drave him,
Adam heard in gentle wise
Allah's whisper, which forgave him :   20
" Go," it said, " from this fair place,
Ye that sinned ; yet not despairing ;
Haply there shall come a grace
And a guidance ; and in fearing
Me, and following My will,   25
Blessed shall your seed be still."

Know ye not that God receives
Gladly back the soul which grieves !
Know ye not that He relents
Ere the sinner well repents ?   30

Terribly His justice burns,
Easily His anger turns.

Spake our Lord : " If one draw near
Unto God—with praise and prayer—
Half a cubit, God will go   5
Twenty leagues to meet him so."

91

" Propitious" is He unto those that show
Compassion to His creatures ; praise Him so.

" No beast of earth, no fowl that flies with wings,"
Saith the great Book, "but is a people, too ;   10
From Allah sprang their life, and unto Him
They shall return : with such heed what ye do !"

There came before our Lord a certain one
Who said, "O Prophet ! as I passed the wood,
I heard the voice of youngling doves which cried,   15
While near the nest their pearl-necked mother cooed."

" Then in my cloth I tied those fledglings twain,
But all the way the mother fluttered nigh ;
See ! she hath followed hither !" Spake our Lord :
"Open thy knotted cloth, and stand thou by."   20

But when she spied her nestlings, from the palm
Down flew the dove, of peril unafeared
So she might succor these. " Seest thou not,"
Our Lord said, " how the heart of this poor bird

"Grows, by her love, greater than his who rides   25
Full-faced against the spear-blades ? thinkest thou
Such fire divine was kindled to be quenched ?
I tell ye nay ! Put back upon the bough

" The nest she claimeth thus.   I tell ye nay !
    From Allah's self cometh this wondrous love :
Yea ! and I swear by Him who sent me here,
    He is more tender then a nursing dove,

" More pitiful to men than she to these.   5
    Therefore fear God in whatsoe'er ye deal
With the dumb peoples of the wing and hoof.
    Yours are they ; yet whene'er ye lift the steel

" To slay for meat, name first the name of God,
    Saying ' Bi 'sm 'illah ! God judge thee and me !   10
God gives thee patience to endure to-day
    The portion that He hath allotted thee.'

" So shall ye eat and sin not ; else the blood
    Crieth against you."   Thus our Prophet spake,
And Islâm doeth it, naming God's name   15
    Before the slaughter,—for that white dove's sake.

By those dumb mouths be ye forgiven,
Ere ye are heard pleading with Heaven.

30

Al-Hâdil !   O " Just Lord !" we magnify
Thy righteous Law, which shall the whole world try.   20

GOD will roll up, when this world's end approacheth,
    The broad blue spangled hangings of the sky,
Even as As-Sigill rolleth up his record,
    And seals and binds it when a man doth die.

---

8. This is the origin of the custom of Muslim hunters and butchers, who
pronounce the formula of excuse and pity before slaying any animal.
23. As-Sigill.—Angel of Registration.

Then the false worshippers, and what they follow,
   Will to the pit, like "stones of hell," descend ;
But true believers shall hear Angels saying,
   "This is your day ; be joyous without end."

In that hour dust shall lie on many faces,   5
   And many faces shall be glad and bright ;
Ye who believe, trust and be patient always,
   Until God judges, for He judges right.

   Give us to pass before Thy throne
   Among the number of Thine own !   10

IV.

With Sa'di[1] in the Garden;

OR,

THE BOOK OF LOVE.

Being the " Ishk "[2] or Third Chapter of the " Bostân"[3] of the Persian poet Sa'di, embodied in a Dialogue held in the Garden of the Taj Mahal,[4] at Agra.[5]

PROEM.

SWEET Friends ! who love the Music of the Sun,
And listened—glad and gracious—many an one,
While, on a light-strung lyre, I sought to tell
Indian Siddartha's wisdom ; . . .

     and to count each golden bead
Of Allah's names of 'Beauty ; . . .   6
      —once more come,
And listen to the Vina and the Drum !
Come once more with me from our somber skies
To hear great Sa'di's tuneful mysteries—   10
" Nightingale of a thousand lays "—for he
Will, 'mid the Garden, sing in many a key

---

1. **Sa'di.**—A Persian poet.
2. **Ishk.**—Passion; love.
3. **Bostan.**—Garden.
4. **Taj Mahal.**—*Taj*, an object of distinguished excellence: *Mahal*, a palace. "Tomb, monuments, screen, walls, and pillars are covered with mosaic work, chiefly of flowers and scrolls, with many passages from the Koran. The scriptural texts are in black marble, but the flowers and scrolls are of jasper, carnelian, agate, and other semi-precious stones, with here and there an addition of mother-of-pearl. We saw a single flower containing more than thirty pieces of stone, and yet the whole flower was not more than an inch in diameter. Bishop Heber says the builders 'designed like Titans and finished like jewelers.' "
5. **Agra.**—A city in the British N. W. Provinces in India.
8. **Vina.**—Hindu musical instrument of the guitar family.

Rare Persian airs.   But, tell them first, my Song !—
Lest they do thee, and me, and Sa'di wrong—
To come with hearts to gentle thoughts inclined,
Since this is only for the wise and kind ;
And, of itself, our Garden shuts its gate   5
On him that's hard, cold, uncompassionate ;
But opens wide its alleys, green and still,
To Sesame of Love and fair Good-will !

TAJ MAHAL.

A passion, and a worship, and a faith
Writ fast in alabaster, so that Earth   10
Hath nothing anywhere of mortal toil
So fine-wrought, so consummate, so supreme—
So, beyond praise, Love's loveliest monument—
As what, in Agra, upon Jumna's bank,
Shah Jahan builded for his Lady's grave.   15
For Mumtaz-i-Mahal, the " Exalted one"—
Queen of her Sultan's heart, and Hindostan—
Here by her Lord and Lover laid to sleep.
And here, too, sleeps the stately King who planned
This splendor for his sorrow—Shah Jahan—   20
Twelve score years back Sultan of India,
Ruler august, and sire of Aurangzebe.

QUEEN ARJAMAND AND THE DAGGER.

Mirza. They tell this story of Queen Arjamand :
So fair she was, so debonair, so wise,
The heart of Shah Jahan slept in her lap :   25
Her mouth issued the King's decrees, her hands
Gave provinces away, and great commands.
No night but at her feet the Emperor
Laid down his cap of lordship and his sword
To take soft counsel from her faithful lips.   30
Which many grudged. . . .

14. **Jumna.**—The principal feeder of the Ganges.

"If we could turn His Majesty," said these,
"From Muntaz, that were well wrought for the State,
Whose banner is become a Persian shift!
Mashallah! will naught dull those dazzling eyes?"
And some one whispered: "Best find newer eyes   5
More dazzling, killing passion with its like;
Since one love-chamber have these hearts of men,
And she who enters thrusts the other forth.
There is that slave-girl, come from Jessulmere,
A brown pearl of the Prophet's Paradise,   10
Wondrously fair—as none e'er saw: give word   ⹁
They deck her with the garments of Muntaz,
And hang the Queen's pearls round her throat, and bring
The Rajpootni into the Queen's own room
When she is gone—so may my lord the King   15
Be tenderly beguiled, and Mumtaz scorned."
And this the Palace Ladies swore was good.
      Saheb. Surely, 'twas perilous?
      Mirza.   Hazrat! the girl
Knew—for they told her—she must die, or gain   20
Life, and long favor, and large wealth in gold,
At moment when her veil should drop, and show
Full moonlight of her face.   To reign, see you,
First in that Court, to win the eyes of him
Who ruled upon the "Peacock-throne," and stretched   25

---

4. **Mashallah.**—"As God wills." [*Shā*, will; and *Allah*.] Expresses wonder or admiration.

9. **Jessulmere.**—A fortified city of Rajpootana, capital of a protected state of the same name.

14. **Rajpoot (Rajput).**—A member of a Hindu race who regard themselves as descendants of the ancient warrior caste—the Aryan race of warriors who established themselves on the lofty table-lands of Hindustan some two thousand years before our era.   The Rajputs claim a descent from the god Rama.   "It is at Oudeypore, above every other city in India, that we find the high representatives of the chief Rajput tribes, and of purest blood, till it has passed into a proverb that 'a courtier of the court of Oudeypore is the model of *bon-ton* for all India.'   This family (of Oudeypore) not only opposed the Mussulman invasion, but they preserved their purity of caste at the cost of blood and treasure, by sundering, during all the Mohammedan rule, every form of connection with the imperial family."

19. **Hazrat.**— A title of honor; a gentleman.

25. **Peacock-throne.**—"The fort or citadel of Delhi had formerly about a dozen large buildings in it, and many small ones; but nearly all of the latter, and some of the former, were destroyed at the time of the Mutiny, or

Hands of command from Balkh to Himalay,
Was worth some risk, it seemed, of fierce farrash.
Therefore—half-willing, half-constrained—she sate
Trembling, upon the silks of Mumtaz' bed,
In vestments of the beauteous Queen, her face 5
Wrapped in the golden chuddur. Oh, 'tis known
What fell, because a Palace maiden heard—
Listening outside the marble jâli-work—
And told it, word for word, to Arjamand.
    Dilazâr. Good Mirza! what befell? 10
    Mirza. The Sultan came
Clad in his private dress—white muslin clasped
With one great pearl, white cap and jeweled shoes—
And, throwing down his scimitar and shawl,
Spake with a gentle smile : "Light of my Life! 15
Once more I shut the great loud world away
And come to reign in this one realm I love,
The heart of Mumtaz !" Rose the Rajpootni,
All quaking underneath her rich disguise,
And bent full lowly to the King of Hind, 20

-----

within a few years after it. The finest of the public ones were preserved,
and they are certainly great curiosities. There are two large halls—the
Dewan-i-Am and the Dewan-i-Khas. The Dewan-i-Khas is smaller than the
other, and is more like a pavilion than a room, being open on three sides.
They say that the ceiling was once composed of gold and silver filigree-
work, made by the jewelers of Delhi ; the same room contained the famous
Peacock-throne. This throne was six feet long by four feet broad, composed of gold inlaid with precious gems. It was surrounded by a gold canopy supported on twelve pillars of the same material, around the canopy
being a fringe of pearls. On each side of the throne stood two umbrellas,
symbols of royalty, formed of crimson velvet richly embroidered with gold
thread and pearls, and with handles of solid gold eight feet long, studded
with diamonds. The back of the throne was a representation of the ex-
panded tail of a peacock, the natural colors of which were imitated by
sapphires, rubies, emeralds, and other precious gems. Its value was esti-
mated, by a French jeweler who saw it, at $30,000,000 It was carried away
by the great Persian conqueror, Nadir Shah, when he captured Delhi in
1738. The place where the throne stood is occupied by a block of marble
bearing the world-famed inscription, 'Agar furduse baru-i-zamin ast, hamin
ast, hamin ast, hamin ast.' (If there be an elysium on earth, it is this, it is
this, it is this).
    2. **Farrash.**—Executioner.
    6. **Chuddur, chuddah.**—In India a square piece of cloth of any kind;
especially the ample sheet commonly worn as a mantle by women in Bengal.
    8. **Jali-work.**—Pierced screen-work, especially in marble or stone,
characteristic of Indian house decoration under Moslem influence.

And kissed his feet ;—then, let her chuddur fall,
And—lo ! it was not Muntaz there ! his Queen !
But that strange, lovely, frightened girl, with throat
Heaving, eyes gleaming, hands on bosom clasped,
Who murmured : " Lord of all the world ! thy slave   5
Waiteth thy will that she may live or die."
   Gulbadan. Doubtless he drew his blade, and slew her there !
   Saheb. He was a man, 'tis writ, of gravity ;
Nice in his pride, terrible in his wrath,
I shudder, Mirza ! for your slave-maiden.   10
   Mirza. Good Sir ! you do not know how fair she was !
Otherwise who had ventured ? On his lips
Ended even in beginning those dread words
Which leaped from royal anger. . . .
                   Allah makes   15
Sometimes a face and form to smite man's soul
With witchery of subtlest symmetry,
And she was such ! . . .
            Nay ! and she marked
The first wrath in the Sultan's countenance   20
Flicker and pass as flame doth pass away
When rain falls on the sparkling of a brand :
So gently dropped upon his mind the rain
Of wonder, pity, will of gentilesse :
And, when she sank upon her face, and sobbed,   25
" Lord of the Age ! forgive me ! send me hence
Alive ! I was not told how great thou art,
How terrible ! how base and bold my deed !"
He raised the Rajpoot girl, gazed on her face
With softening eyes, and, while her heart beat quick,   30
Spake : " Get thee hence alive ! Fairest thou art
Of Allah's works. . . .
Yet one thing fairer is than even thou,
And sweeter far for me to have and keep,
The faith I held and hold to her whose name   35
Thou art not meet to hear ! Begone ! begone !"

Saheb. Right royal ! and nowise of the Mogul type,
As I have read.   What next befell that slave,
With respite of eye-wink ?
Mirza.   She glided forth,
Seeking escape ; but those that heard the words   5
And saw all done, laid hands on her, and haled
The weeping maid to angry Arjamand,
Dressed as she was in the Queen's cloth of gold,
Wearing the Palace-pearls, ungirt, new-bathed,
Painted, and henna-stained, and scented sweet.   10
They told what passed, and how the Sultan spake,
She cowering at the proud Sultana's foot.
Dilhazâr. Then the Queen stabbed her to the heart—was't
    not ?
Straight to the heart !   Wallah ! I would have stabbed !
Mirza. Then the Queen drew the dagger from her waist, 15
A knife of watered steel, hafted with jade,
And on the hilt a ruby worth three lackhs,
Pigeon-blood color, marvelous, the gift
Of Shah Jahan in some soft hour of love—
An unmatched stone.   And, when they looked to see   20
The keen point pierce the panting satin skin
Stripped of its veil—Arjamand stooped and placed
The dagger blade beneath her sandal, snapped
The bright steel short, and, drawing near to hers
That Rajpoot's face, kissed tenderly her mouth,   25
And gravely spake : " Go ! thou hast given me
The richest, best, last gift which Earth could give

---

1. **Moguls.**—Mongols were called Moguls by the Persians. " The Mongols correspond in almost every respect with the Turanian family.   They include Chinese, Indo-Chinese, Tartars of all kinds, Burmese, Lapps, Finns, Esquimaux Siamese, Tibetans, Turks, and even Magyars.   Collectively they are the great Nomadic people of the earth."
10. **Henna.**—A shrub growing in moist situations throughout the north of Africa, Arabia, Persia, and the E. Indies.   The leaves abound in coloring matter, and are very generally used by the women of the East in staining the nails and tips of the fingers of an orange color.
14. **Walla, wallah.**—Fellow; man; doer; agent; a civil servant, selected by competitive examination.
16. **Hafted with jade,**—*Haft.* a handle as of a knife or dagger; *jade,* a mineral of a greenish color, used by natives for weapons.
17. **Lackh, lac.**—The sum of 100,000—usually of rupees.

In comfort of my great Lord's constancy.
Take thou this jewel of my dagger, Friend !—
Nowise its point !—and a Queen's thanks therewith
For treason dearly done to Arjamand !"

So passed the Rajpoot, rich and scatheless, thence.   5

    Saheb. Sweeter her memory seems for that one deed
Of loftiest clemency than for her face
Of heavenly charm, or for her sovereignties,
Or fame or tomb !   How think you, Gulbadan ?

V.

Lotus and Jewel.

" A Rajpût Nurse."

" Whose tomb have they builded, Vittoo ! under this tamarind
tree,
With its door of the rose-veined marble, and white dome
stately to see,
Was he holy Brahman, or Yogi, or Chief of the Rajpût line,
Whose urn rests here by the river, in the shade of the beautiful
shrine ?"

" May it please you," quoth Vittoo, salaaming, " Protector of
all the poor !   5
It was not for holy Brahman they carved that delicate door ;
Nor for Yogi, nor Rajpût Rana, built they this gem of our
land ;
But to tell of a Rajpût woman, as long as the stones should
stand.

" Her name was Môti, the pearl-name ; 'twas far in the
ancient times ;
But her moon-like face and her teeth of pearl are sung of still
in our rhymes ;   10
And because she was young, and comely, and of good repute,
and had laid
A babe in the arms of her husband, the Palace-Nurse she was
made :

---

3. **Brahman.**—Priest. Brahma, one of the three chief gods of Hindu
pantheon, especially associated with the function of creation.
3. **Yogi.**—A devotee of the Yoga system of philosophy. *Yoga*, a species
of asceticism among the Hindus.
3. **Rajpût.**—A member of a Hindu race who regarded themselves as descendants of the ancient warrior caste. They now chiefly occupy Rajpootana.
12. " A Hindu father acknowledges paternity by receiving in his arms his
new-born child."

" For the sweet chief-queen of the Rana in Joudhpore city
  had died,
Leaving a motherless infant, the heir to that race of pride ;
The heir of the peacock-banner, of the five-colored flag, of the
  throne
Which traces its record of glory from days when it ruled
  alone ;

" From times when, forth from the sunlight, the first of our
  kings came down   5
And had the earth for his footstool, and wore the,stars for his
  crown,
As all good Rajpûts have told us.; so Môti was proud and true,
With the Prince of the land on her bosom, and her own brown
  baby too.

"And the Rajpût woman will have it (I know not myself of
  these things)
As the two babes lay on her lap there, her lord's, and the
  Joudhpore King's ;   10
So loyal was the blood of her body, so fast the faith of her
  heart,
It passed to her new-born infant, who took of her trust its
  part.

" He would not suck of the breast-milk till the Prince had
  drunken his fill ;   .
He would not sleep to the cradle-song till the Prince was
  lulled and still ;
And he lay at night with his small arms clasped round the
  Rana's child,   15
As if those hands like the rose-leaf could shelter from treason
  wild.

---

5. The Rajpût dynasty is said to be descended from the Sun.
10. Joudhpore.—A city in Rajpootana, capital of a protected state of
the same name.
15. Rana.—King.

"For treason was wild in the country, and villainous men
    had sought
The life of the heir of the gadi, to the Palace in secret
    brought ;
With bribes to the base, and with knife-thrusts for the faith-
    ful, they made their way
Through the line of the guards, and the gateways, to the hall
    where the women lay.

" There Môti, the foster-mother, sat singing the children to
    rest,   5
Her baby at play on her crossed knees, and the King's son
    held to her breast ;
And the dark slave-maidens round her beat low on the cym-
    bal's skin
Keeping the time of her soft song—when—Saheb !—there
    hurried in

" A breathless watcher, who whispered, with horror in eyes
    and face :
' Oh ! Môti ! men come to murder my Lord the Prince in this
    place !   10
They have bought the help of the gate-guards, or slaughtered
    them unawares,
Hark ! that is the noise of their tulwars, the clatter upon the
    stairs ! '

" For one breath she caught her baby from her lap to her
    heart, and let
The King's child sink from her nipple, with lips still clinging
    and wet,
Then tore from the Prince his head-cloth, and the putta of
    pearls from his waist,   15
And bound the belt on her infant, and the cap on his brows,
    in haste ;

---

2. **Gadi.**—The throne.
8. **Saheb, sahib.**—Sir; gentleman.
12. **Tulwars.**—Indian swords.
15. **Putta.**—Belt.

" And laid her own dear offspring, her flesh and blood on the
    floor,
With the girdle of pearls around him, and the cap that the
    King's son wore ;
While close to her heart, which was breaking, she folded the
    Râja's joy,
And—even as the murderers lifted the purdah—she fled with
    his boy.

" But there (so they deemed) in his jewels, lay the Chota
    Rana, the Heir ;   5
'The cow with two calves has escaped us,' cried one, ' it is
    right and fair
She should save her own butcha ; no matter ! the edge of the
    dagger ends
This spark of Lord Raghoba's sunlight ; stab thrice and four
    times, O friends ! '

" And the Rajpût women will have it (I know not if this can
    be so)
That Môti's son in the putta and golden cap cooed low,   10
When the sharp blades met in his small heart, with never one
    moan or wince,
But died with a babe's light laughter, because he died for his
    Prince.

" Thereby did that Rajpût mother preserve the line of our
    Kings."
"Oh ! Vittoo," I said, "but they gave her much gold and
    beautiful things,

---

3. **Raja, rajah.**—A native prince or king.
4. **Purdah.**—A curtain.
5. **Chota Rana.**—" Little King."
7. **Butcha.**—" Little one."
8. **Lord Raghoba.**—A celebrated king of Oude, descended from the
Sun.

And garments, and land for her people, and a home in the
    Palace ! May be
She had grown to love that Princeling even more than the
    child on her knee."

" May it please the Presence ! " quoth Vittoo, " it seemeth not
    so ! They gave
The gold and the garments and jewels, as much as the proud-
    est would have ;
But the same night deep in her true heart she buried a knife,
    and smiled,   5
Saying this : ' I have saved my Rana ! I must go to suckle
    my child ! ' "

VI.

Miscellaneous Poems.

SHE AND HE.

"SHE is dead!" they said to him.   "Come away;
Kiss her! and leave her!—thy love is clay!"

They smoothed her tresses of dark-brown hair;
On her forehead of marble they laid it fair:

Over her eyes, which gazed too much,   5
They drew the lids with a gentle touch;

With a tender touch they closed up well
The sweet thin lips that had secrets to tell;

About her brows, and her dear, pale face
They tied her veil and her marriage-lace;   10

And drew on her white feet her white silk shoes;—
Which were the whiter no eye could choose!

And over her bosom they crossed her hands;
"Come away," they said,—"God understands!"

And then there was Silence;—and nothing there   15
But the Silence—and scents of eglantere,

And jasmine, and roses, and rosemary;
For they said, "As a lady should lie, lies she!"

And they held their breath as they left the room,
With a shudder to glance at its stillness and gloom.   20

But he—who loved her too well to dread
The sweet, the stately, the beautiful dead,—

He lit his lamp, and took the key,
And turn'd it !—alone again—he and she !

He and she ; but she would not speak,
Though he kissed, in the old place, the quiet cheek ;

He and she ; yet she would not smile, 5
Though he call'd her the name that was fondest erewhile.

He and she ; and she did not move
To any one passionate whisper of love !

Then he said, " Cold lips ! and breast without breath !
Is there no voice ?—no language of death 10

" Dumb to the ear and still to the sense,
But to heart and to soul distinct,—intense ?

" See, now,—I listen with soul, not ear—
What was the secret of dying, Dear ?

" Was it the infinite wonder of all, 15
That you ever could let life's flower fall ?

" Or was it a greater marvel to feel
The perfect calm o'er the agony steal ?

" Was the miracle greatest to find how deep,
Beyond all dreams, sank downward that sleep ? 20

" Did life roll backward its record, Dear,
And show, as they say it does, past things clear ?

" And was it the innermost heart of the bliss
To find out so what a wisdom love is ?

" Oh, perfect Dead ! oh, Dead most dear, 25
I hold the breath of my soul to hear ;

" I listen—as deep as to horrible hell,
    As high as to heaven !—and you do not tell !

" There must be pleasures in dying, Sweet,
    To make you so placid from head to feet !

" I would tell *you*, Darling, if I were dead,   5
    And 'twere your hot tears upon *my* brow shed.

" I would say, though the angel of death had laid
    His sword on my lips to keep it unsaid.

" *You* should not ask, vainly, with streaming eyes,
    Which in Death's touch was the chiefest surprise ;   10

" The very strangest and suddenest thing
    Of all the surprises that dying must bring."

Ah ! foolish world ! Oh ! most kind Dead !
    Though he told me, who will believe it was said ?

Who will believe that he heard her say,   15
    With the soft rich voice, in the dear old way :—

" The utmost wonder is this,—I hear,
    And see you, and love you, and kiss you, Dear ;

" I can speak, now you listen with soul alone ;
    If your soul could see, it would all be shown   20

" What a strange delicious amazement is Death,
    To be without body and breathe without breath.

" I should laugh for joy if you did not cry ;
    Oh, listen ! love lasts !—love never will die.

" I am only your Angel who was your Bride ;   25
    And I know, that though dead, I have never died."

www.ingramcontent.com/pod-product-compliance
Lightning Source LLC
Chambersburg PA
CBHW021554270326
41931CB00009B/1211